WAKE UP HUMANITY!

Poems About You and Me

Elsa Mendoza

ISBN-13: 978-1721193493

ISBN-10: 1721193499

Also by
Elsa Mendoza

YOU CAN QUOTE ME ON THIS

**Words to Empower You
and Awaken Your Consciousness**

INTRODUCTION

Dear Humans,

I am one of those who hope for a better world. I am one of those who desire unity and love amongst all of us. I am one of those who seek harmony and peace in humanity. I am one of those who realized that I am not just here on earth to live, work and die. I am not just a pack of neurons. No, I am more than this.

I am one of those who realized that I am a spiritual being just having the human experience on this planet. I am one of those who is also aware that our planet, our world, the entire universe is working perfectly for our benefit regardless of any situation.

I stand along speakers, authors, bloggers, seekers, thinkers, movers, influencers of the world who talk about this very same subject albeit in different ways but with the same intention.

This book is a collection of poems based on my realizations, awareness and life experiences in my spiritual journey and observations on humanity. Humanity is a vast subject. It covers a multitude of topics, concerns and questions. This book touches some of these: our true nature, beliefs, challenges, relationships, and behavior toward each other.

We have witnessed and experienced the results of our achievements, success, failures and the effects of our conscious and unconscious actions. Some of you might even question why our past challenges are still challenges to this date. We somehow could not get our desired results no matter how much we try. We have separation beliefs causing dis-alignment with our higher selves-our innermost being.

The message of this book is for you to remember that we are people of power, peace, joy, abundance and most of all love. I have written and sent the same message in my first book consisting of encouraging, empowering and thought provoking quotes. Now I write to you in free-verse poems. Just a caveat, I am not a professional poet, nor do I say that I am an expert when it comes to poems. Poetry for me is one of my expressions in writing. My purpose is not to impose on you as readers, but as you are an important part of humanity, I would like to invite each one of you to pause, reflect and ask yourselves what kind of a source or a contributor you are in the collective consciousness and the betterment of humanity.

Peace, blessings and love,

Elsa Mendoza, CCC
Long Beach, CA

Readers my dearest,
My second book I present to you
I write to you in poems
With some rhymes
and stanzas I reach out to you
Humanity is my best pick
My heart pounds as I think of it
In some you may find your truth
Where some you will
remember your youth
At times you might awaken
Or you may be shaken
Change if you must
First your thoughts if you trust
Review your beliefs if you can
Awaken the species from your end
I encourage each man
To remember the real you again
In unity, equality we live,
love and stand again
In one voice we sing God's love song
In one world and oneness we belong

DEDICATION

I lovingly dedicate this book to the lovers
of mankind, to the seekers of truth and
to the bringers of light-to humanity.

CONTENTS

IN THE BEGINNING

GOD

In unison we say,
God is
The Creator, the Ruler
The King, the Knowing
The Heavens above, the Love

And others say,
There is nothing
There might be something
Probably, perhaps
Who knows? I don't know
Do you know?

And I say,
The up and the down
The left and the right
The male and the female
The love and the hate
The good and the bad
The light and the darkness
The great unseen
The you and the me
The Magnificent Everything
The Divine Intelligent Designer
My Infinite Creator
My Everything, my Knowing
My Experience, my Source
My Guide, my Wisdom
My All, in me
I Am

What do you say?

THE ALL

God
The three letters
That rule for the better
The one word
Written, uttered, and used to one's accord

Some said the All is He
Some said She
Some said either
Some said neither

Some call the All Christ
For some,
Buddha, Allah, Krishna
The Divine
The Synonym of Love
The Universe
The Mighty Designer
The Divine Power and Intelligence

Some believe in the All's existence
And some are still caught up in resistance
Some created and based the All
in the image of human concept
Some think that it's just another precept
I say the All is individualized
Until everyone realized

UNIVERSE

One lovely night
Through the window
I was gazing up above
I see billions of stars twinkling
The big moon shining
The past staring
The history of creation
From nothing to something

Is this just a probability?
Is it a possibility? I asked
No, my heart replied
It is vastness
It is God
Evolving, expanding,
Growing, loving
Galaxies, planets,
Atoms, molecules
Energy flowing
Vibrations, frequencies
Fields of consciousness
Dwelling
Beings
Humans
In us
We are

THE PLACE CALLED EARTH

Created complete
Majestic and neat
Wonderful, colorful
Bountiful, beautiful
Endlessly provides to all in full

Nobody can declare the earth
is his ownership
It's a must to establish a partnership
The place called earth can exist on its own
It can stand alone, thrive, and survive strong

Mysterious she can be
So we should be ready
The surprise is sometimes a catastrophe
Her message is clear
That we should hear
Lessons we can adhere

Our actions are crucial
Do not wait for another comeback
To Mother Earth we should care
and give back
As she always has our back

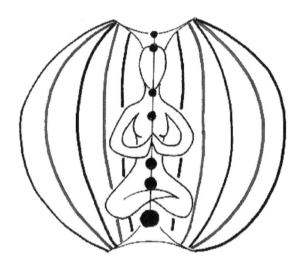

ONE WITH GOD

Sent to earth with glee
By God we all agree
Lost in the midst to see
To God I sent my plea

Remember who you are
God said in that hour
You are love and Me
I ask what, who, why me?
Look around you, look at Me
From love, I created you
From my image and likeness, I formed you
You come from Me
You are love and Me
Said by God, we all agree

My life experience taught me
to believe and see
I remembered me
I am one with thee
One with all
As God is you, me, and all

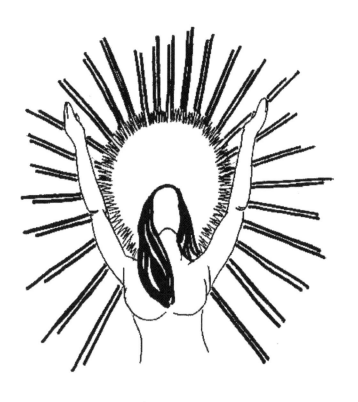

YOU ARE THE
LIGHT AND SOUL

You are a non-physical and a physical being
You are a spirit and a soul
You are called the light
and one with the Divinity
Sent to earth and multiplied to individuality
To experience humanity

In the world of duality
the light experienced darkness
That it can again be brightness
The purpose is to experience
the self and the essence
Of the ever best Presence

The soul has no care
for our earthly achievements
Or any of our earthly contentment
Beingness, unity and perfect love
Is only what it is after to have

It is always seeking
To be like our King
Through the roaming in darkness
Light then found love and forgiveness
And realized that it is all its trueness

ABOUT YOU
AND ME

HUMANITY

There is so much more of who we are
Who and what we know of ourselves
We are atoms and molecules
Stardust compacted in earth-suits
The collective consciousness
The physical extension of the source energy
The source that is Divine that is God
The deliberate creators of reality
We are beyond our physical bodies
Gods and Goddesses
Born as Jesus, Buddha, Allah,
Krishna, and Zoroaster
We are the light of the world, a holy nation

With our thoughts we can create
With our words the course of life can change
With our emotions we can be guided
With our vibrations and energies
we can be united

We are the peace and hope
that we all long for
We are the joy for which we yearn
We are the love that we desire
We are the answer to a better world

The power in we

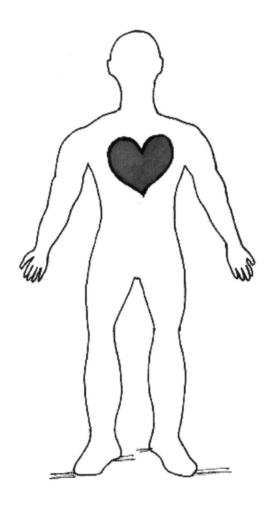

THE REAL ME

Skin, bones, muscles in my body
Senses I use in humanity
Rise, eat, work, live and repeat daily
Is this all really me?

Fame and fortune
Prestige in titles
Appreciation in recognition
Really is this just me?

Sleeper I have been
A wanderer in the dim
Life's challenges have me awakened
Abounding wisdom I've been enlightened

My questions have been answered
The darkness turned into brightness
The unsettling noise has been silenced
My wretchedness is now happiness
My madness became peacefulness

Conscious I have become
In spirit I come
I am an observer of my thoughts
I am not my name, image,
beliefs or my things
I am more than just being a human
I am a healer, a restorer, a peacemaker
and a lover to man
I am the loving awareness

GOD AND ME

I asked when I was five
Who is this God?
Where is God?
I was told by many to look up above
In a white robe and beard I will see Him
With wrath and judgment
As punishment I will feel
By my disobedience I should then fear
Though this God has unconditional love

I asked again when I was twenty-five
Who is this God?
Where is God?
In my longing and yearning on thirty-five
I found God
I found myself
It's just all Love

I asked once more at forty-five
Who is this God?
Where is God?
Everywhere I look
Anything I hear
The answer is...
...I AM

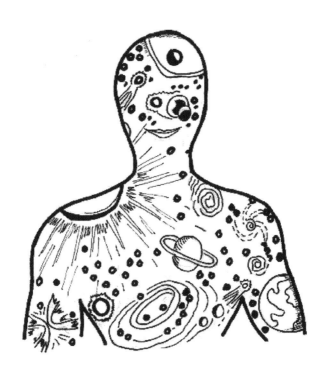

THE UNIVERSE IN ME

Big Bang!
The theory and history began
From the star it started
Everything exploded and parted

Came the first sentient beings
Then came us human beings
Called the highest form of creation
But our ways are still of a primitive nation
Primitive that we are still in separation
Unaware that we are one heavenly nation

Stardust I find
Elements also in body of mine
No more mysteries behind
Beauty and wonders are divine
I pondered if it is just a dwelling
I realized that it's just me in living
I am the Universe and the Universe is in me

FEELINGS AND INTUITION

Some days are merry
Other days are dreary
Few days are blue
Next days are true

There are days of mundane
And days of insane
Oh these feelings of tide
What you are is a ride
Sometimes you are a guide
And guide as you are
Right is always what you are

Some said you are just emotions
Some said you are intuition
Either/or - I like your game
I listen and follow just the same
So I am forever in your lane

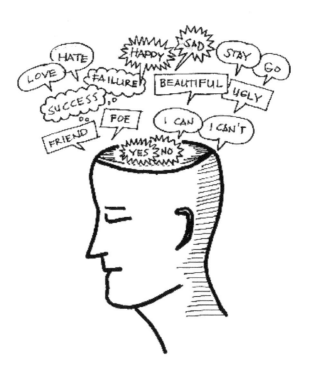

THE THOUGHTS SPEAK

Fifty to seventy thousand numbers
are my daily grind
Staying in the human mind I am inclined
I am always active
So I can be captive

Some can easily be consumed
Some just cannot be doomed
Others are just master observers
The rest are just sleepers and consumers

Once I get processed
In repetition I get to progress
A belief then is born
And it's up to them to scorn
Choose wisely if you must
It affects your life, as you trust

PURPOSE

I roam
I groan
I moan
I search
I purge

Oh, what shall I do?
A doctor perhaps
An actor in the workshop
A pastor maybe
A dictator probably

Long after the overstretched journey
And the meander to different paths
to eternity
Is just an endless and joyful creativity
To decide, to declare, to live
To express anew the different versions of me

MY OTHER ME

Contrast is our world
And our choices are gold
Everyday is a yay or a nay
What and who am I for today

Power and greatness I desire
To be right among others, I aspire
To the fullest of my extent
Hurting others to my mend
As long as I am the one famous in the end

My other me is hungry
Always satisfaction-thirsty
Just lonely
And in some days, needy

Should I hate you,
Maintain you,
Or embrace you?

Accept you I must do
As you help me choose too
Remember who I truly am;
The opposite of you

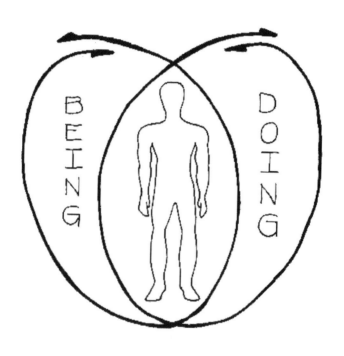

HUMAN BEING OR
HUMAN DOING

The beingness of the sun
It rises and sets
To give light and energy
The beingness of the oceans
It is consistent in providing water and food

All sentient beings
Its purpose is just to be
Just like the plants, flowers and the trees
They grow, blossom and bear fruit
To give oxygen, healing and food
Just like the animals
They go through the life cycle
from birth till death
To multiply, survive and
cohabitate with nature

In harmony, these sentients live
Then came the human beings,
the highest form considered
The one that really mattered,
"Is it the highest?" some beings asked
Then why the certain act, always doing, forgetting to be
being

Said the other beings,
Oh, these human beings
Destruction is a must
Serving their greed is a task
We lost our homes and friends
from their doings
On earth we then ask, should they,
really be living?

OUR CHALLENGES

RELATIONSHIPS

It is the meeting of the minds
Connected by attraction
Expression of care
Nurtured by affection
Secured by commitment
Shielded by love
Comes in sorts
Grows on hope
Expires on desertion
Where humanity has a fixation
So fixed that some could not move on

It shapes the world
Changes people
Comforts and teaches
Affects all lives
Links us all

Men of the loving,
A must to remember
Perfectly you were created
Complete you have always been

Relationships with others
can sometimes wither
The relationship with yourself
you have to utmost consider
As a relationship's only purpose
Is to share your completeness with the other
Is for you to know and for you to find

Which part of you will show up
during its term

You as a co-creator
You have the power to control
You can lovingly create
Or you can destructively end

FAMILY

Some are small and some are huge
The foundation of our youth
The source of some of our truth
Called the city of our refuge

By blood a pact was made
With one name we're all the same
The rules we all follow
In love we all grow

Father, mother,
Sister and brother
The roots of our known identity
Our little society
The foundation of our entire nation

The journey is sometimes smooth
One day can also be tempestuous
Care as best as you can
Cherish it till the end

FRIENDSHIP

I have said before
To few people and more
That friendship can only be defined
Then can be refined
By one's very experience
And not by expectation

Strangers when it started
From days to centuries
These strangers have expanded
From comrades to families

For some this link can die
When the mind stops to rely
For some this link can grow
When the heart starts to further know

Friendship is such a gift
That nourishes our spirits
As stewards of these gifts
In prayer to God we should always lift

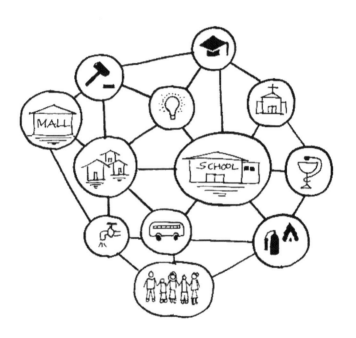

SOCIETY

For many centuries
We all gathered and formed
With one belief and goal
We communed at our best
To create order, maintain justice, and peace

Do you remember the rules
that were passed?
Have you read the history?
Do you remember our triumphs
and achievements?
What about our defeats and challenges?

Observe our current state
Have we progressed from the past?
Have we learned from our mistakes?
Racism, hunger, poverty, greed,
Injustice and even more are still existent

What happened to the rules created?
What happened to our choices?
What happened to love?
What happened to us?

BUSINESS

For not all but many
It's all about the money
Not everyone admits to the many

For not all but many
It is about service
True results, however, surface

For not all but many
Greed is their mission
To get more is the compulsion

For not all but many
Ads are concealed by comforting lies
Causing others to expire

For not all but many
The desire to quick wealth
Puts at stake one's health

For not all but many
The yearning for fame
Sometimes ends in shame

Oh you few from the many
Let your honesty, integrity shine more
Let your service and love
inspire these many, if not all

BELIEFS

In its simplicity,
Our thoughts that we continue to think
become our reality

In its complexity,
The imposed ones brings dis-alignment
with our higher selves

In its beauty,
Our free will gives us a choice with
what works and serves our purpose

In the reality that we know,
We sometimes blindly follow, so blind
we no longer think anymore

Rulers and leaders,
Let your beliefs and instructions bring
peace and hope in our planet

Gurus and shamans,
Let your beliefs and wisdoms bring
more joy, healing and enlightenment

Pope, bishops, ministers and rabbis,
Let your beliefs and teachings bring
more love and unity on earth

Men of this earth,
May your beliefs align with your own truth

LIFE

A game and a cycle you are
Up and down every hour
The belief is you are short
I say only if you support

In free will I create my reality
I ask if there is a guarantee
As I create
You gravitate and elevate
You let me see what I'd like to see
That there is only one permanency
Change is always present in me

It is what we make it they say
I believe in the hearsay
You are not to be wasted, I pray
But to be appreciated always

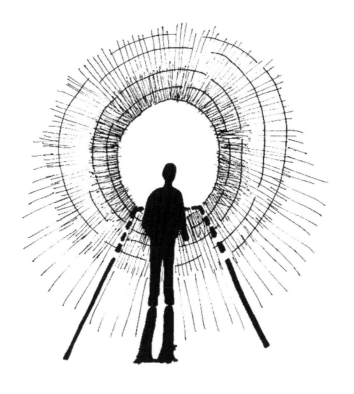

THE DEATH YOU THINK

It may come in a surprise
It may come as a plan
Sometimes it can drag
Other times one can rush

No age, no gender
No one is spared
Some are terrified
Some just surrender the fight

The living said, grief is so heavy
The pain is such agony
Replaying a memory
Serve to remedy

This death is not what you think
It can change in a blink
It's a cycle if you remember
It's a start if you discover

The bodies can decay
The memories can fade away
Spirits are who we really are
Eternal beings are what we are

From peace we come
To peace we will return
To say rest in peace is no longer needed
Live in peace and celebrate death instead
We came as souls, and as souls
we end up again
Death you are not the end,
But an awakening and a beginning so far

RELIGION

The past millennia, decades, and centuries
Systems of worship and faith were created
Rules and structures were laid out
To recognize and revere the loving Deity
To teach about love for one another
To unite mankind and achieve world peace
To some, to attain salvation from hell

Fast forward to present
These systems are still existent
Rules and structures unchanged
Men are still confused about the Deity
More are lost in their true nature of selves
Some are unclear why they need to be saved
Hatred still overpowers love
Men are still divided

There are many faiths, other religions said
But one God, one path, and one church, some declared
Confusion, conflict, and even wars happened
Separation continues amongst nations and men
Sinners we are still called
In hell we are still on hold
Truth has yet to be told

What happened to
these faith-based systems?
What happened to
the teachings about unity and love?

Why are men in fear of
the unconditional loving God?
Why do men still question
who they really are?
Why do men need to be saved,
from where, from whom?
Why are men still judged
if born out of love and from love?
Why are men labeled sinners at birth
if their origin is perfection and love?

Leaders of these systems
listen to the questions of men
The universe endlessly expands and changes
Seasons and generations change
But some religious teachings never change
Men still search for their true nature
Men unceasingly separate themselves
from one another
Men still think they are separate from God

POLITICS

Men in suits and ties
May look very nice
Candidates in debates
Voters fall in love or in hate

Day of election
People in power in selection
Wondering and worrying
The victor among the candidates

Now it has begun
Your bet won
Your joy a ton
It's showtime
And in no time
Your bet's promises broken
Your heart betrayed
Your hopes ruined

Lawmakers and other rulers
The promises you have made
They're bound to be fulfilled
You come up with rules
That people no longer believe
No more blind eyes and deaf ears
For these have been done in several years

Why can't equality, justice,
and peace be fully achieved?

Aren't you all tired of the
old game of shame?
What is taking you all so long to unite?
Are your personal interests
and businesses at stake?
Or are your egos in each other's way?

EDUCATION

Too many subjects being taught
But not all are useful in life
Too much information transmitted
But not all are important
Too many lecturing hours in the classroom
But less time to apply and experience them
Too much knowledge gained
But less values learned

Too much material for memorization
But less comprehension
Too much setting of instructions and rules
But less focus on student's opinions
and their questions
Too many exams to test one's knowledge
But only few are needed
Too much focus on the test results
But less on the ability and creativity

Too many charges on tuition fees
Fewer people have access to learn
Too many schools run on a tight budget
Illiterate population soaring
Too many teachings from
the old fixed mindset system
People have become
more like followers and robots
Instead of thinkers, innovators and creators
Generations have passed
and times have changed
The old systems are evidently failing
Is this the kind of education we offer
to the future leaders of our planet?

WAR

Of all the human-made
This is such an enormous waste
The early millennia to present date
It has never ceased, never ends,
and it's always in haste

Initialized by two
Followed by a few
Agreed by many
Till everyone is ready

A journey has begun
For the patriotic uniformed men
Bloodbath here
Lives lost there
Pain here
Glory there
A cycle of debacle

A story has started
A history recorded
A journey ended
Families comforted
The few good uniformed men
Were no longer founded

Humans, what have you earned?
Humans, when is the end?
Humans, when will you mend?
Humans, when will you learn?

TERRORISM

People killing in the name of a god
Students shot down in cold blood
Buildings crumble, villages ransacked
Innocent ones hostaged,
entire town terrorized

Terrorism
It arises anytime
From anyone
From anywhere
From anything

It ignites war
Fighting for a specific cause
For someone's belief
For someone's pain

It is a distorted perception of love
resulting in fear
For a country's rights being taken away
For someone's beloved
suffering from injustice
For a threat that may or may not transpire

It calls for change
A call to reflect
A call to unite
A call to love one another again

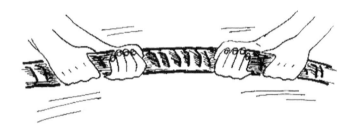

COMPETITION

I am different than others
I am better than others
I am always right over others
I should be, it should be

I must have
I should have
I better have
I have to prove
As I am the only one who can have

Who are you?
What are you?
What do you have?
What can you prove?
The ego said and asked

It's good for self-discovery
Great for self-improvement
Best for self-empowerment
Agreed by the ego and society

Programmed, conditioned and wired
We believed and got mired
Blind and asleep we have decided
A tiring cycle we have all accepted
Wake up, give up,
we are in no competition with anyone
As you and I are equal, special, and one

ATTACHMENTS

We love our things
What it offers us
Our success and dreams
How it excites us
Our relationships
How it satisfies us
Our created self-image
How people praise us

In time, our things got old and rusty
Our relationships withered and died
Our true identities were forgotten
We were left lost, confused, and shaken
We thought we should just die

We have forgotten that there are
more than all these things
That life is not just about
success and dreams
That relationships can transform
That we are more than
the self-concept that we know
That attachment is not permanent
We have forgotten that change
is the only permanent thing

LABELS

On a sunny day
She wears her favorite red dress
Mid-knee-length that curved
with her voluptuous body
As she walks
She is called, "Whore!" "Slut!" "Cunt!"
She just survived a divorce

On the same day
Comes another human, in same dress
Mid-knee-length
As this human walks
Someone shouts, "Raging faggot!"
He came out just to be himself

A young lad in school
Cute and a little chubby
At the last row, a kid shouted
"Fat face!" "Pig!" Snort, snort
The young lad gained weight
due to an illness

A new look
A satisfied woman strolling at the park
With new breast implants
'Hey Barbie, come and get me!"
called the spectators
She just survived breast cancer

Name calling, labeling,
Bullying, judging
Is this necessary?
Does it satisfy you?
Does it heal your pain too?

DISCRIMINATION

From the early centuries
To our present time
Men's love for superiority
Is still in authority

Men's hunger for power
Has set them asunder
They will do anything
To satisfy their whims

The belief of separation
Created discrimination
In age, gender, ethnicity
Beliefs and disability

Men's lack of self-love
Has caused them hatred
They see and feel judgment
Ends in a predicament

Men, it is time to be more compassionate
It is time to be much kinder
It is time to be more accepting
It is time to love yourselves once more
It is time to love each other again

ESSENTIALS

In my early teenage years,
usually before the day starts to heat up
An old bag lady would sit at our front porch and would
set her stuff up
She would sit hugging her skinny legs
and her back leaned on the wall
I would hear her sing and talk to herself
with no care at all

From our living room, I would see her
Her presence made me excited
to go out and watch her
Her scruffy clothes and foul smell
did not bother me
Hearing her songs and stories of war intrigued me

Her smile and laughter
were a combination of joy and pain
Her songs were the memories
she experienced and gained
My mom would hand her pieces of bread
and tall glass of coffee
So the bag lady can tell stories
and sing more for free

Decades have passed
and I moved to different places
From time to time
I still remember the bag lady

I can still picture her tired, wrinkled
but smiling face
I can still hear her cries
for her lost love and her family

The bag lady is just like you and me,
who has basic survival needs
She is the result of
the problem we have ignored
Society has transformed from
beliefs of unity to beliefs of separation
It's the survival of the fittest and senseless competition
that should no longer go on

Food, shelter, clothing
is every human's essential need
It is humanity's concern,
but not all have access to it
Food, shelter, clothing -
some have more than enough
Others barely enough -
the rest have nothing at all

Food, shelter, clothing, a must for humanity
Not just an entitlement to some
What are we doing?
Why are we ignoring?

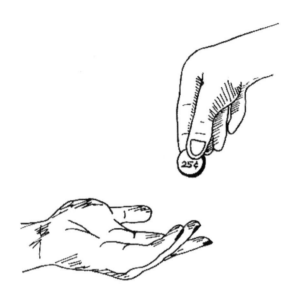

POVERTY

The greed of the rulers
Has robbed many pockets
Has made thieves and robbers
Has caused hunger in families

The system of the world
Only works for a few
Hopeful for some
Unfair for many

What then is the key?
To benefit the many
Empowerment, equality
Or the commitment to help

The choices of men
In times of plenty
Lavishness and vices
They squander their fortunes
In times of want
Attachments to material desires
They end up penniless and depressed

Men, let your choices be wise
Rulers and leaders
Let the voices of the many
Be heard and be justified
For decades, these voices have been denied

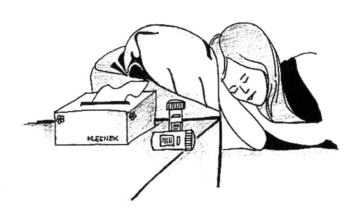

ILLNESSES

Some were purposely created
Announce the epidemic to the public
Media to persuade
Medical team dismayed
Spread the virus
Let them be in dis-ease
Pharma business to the boom

Some you unconsciously allowed
Unaware of the stress that consumed you
The resistances in life you have made
The fear that traumatized you
The anxiousness that almost killed you
You may not realize
It is just you
The source of all your dis-eases

Men be awakened
Say no more to fake healers
Evoke your self-healing powers
Go back to the fundamentals
Embrace the naturals

WASTE

Air, noise, trash pollution
Complain, blame, and confusion
Weather to the extremes
Environment to the grim
Why is this happening?
What are we doing?

How lucky we are
We have a place to live
We could breathe the air for free
We could enjoy the oceans and seas

But how could it be
We can't let the earth just be
We take its provisions for granted
We damage it with our ignorance and greed
As if it is our own property

Is it laziness?
Perhaps carelessness
Could be a habit
Probably acquired
Maybe ignorance
What can it be?

How many more catastrophes?
How many more deaths?
How many more illnesses
Does humanity have to endure
To let the earth be as it used to be?

MEDIA

With one blow in print
Some would know
With one broadcast in the radio
Many would know
With one air on TV show
The entire world knows
News in a flash
Suddenly topics discussed
The world reacts
Either to believe them or not

The gullible said, oh no
The skeptics said, yeah right
The complacent said nothing at all
Neither, either, or
Media is just all show
Where one can be built with words of truth
And some can be destroyed
with words of lies

People behind media
Your news is vital
The world is shaped by our beliefs
You can capitalize or profit from these
Or you can create a world of peace

DRUGS

A useless continuous war
Decades of eradication
Far from dissolution
Officers in charge
Are either foolish
Or just feigning to be
As profits are fifty–fifty
So eyes became blind
Ears became deaf
Hands became tied

Decades of supply
Demand is high
Drug lord's happy sigh
His associates in greed
Benefit from people's pain and need
Relationships, livelihoods, and well-being
Broken, lost, and debilitated
People left addicted
Profiteers more abusive

Another epic of humanity's pick
When are we deciding to end this story?
When are we deciding
to fully obliterate this challenge?
When are we deciding
that enough is truly enough?

HUMAN TRAFFICKING

A man with a vision
A hope and aspiration
Out of desperation
Took a destination
To the land of milk and honey
The land of opportunity

Arrived at the promised land
Welcomed by crooks
More desperation at hand
He lived in a box with other men
Little means of survival
The wait is excruciating
Ends up in a sweatshop

A woman with the same vision
Same hope and aspiration
At the promised land
Met up with the other women
She was forced in her weakness
Drugged and raped
Ends up in prostitution

Fear and greed
The ongoing motivation
Became the society's creed
Oh, holy nation
People are in dire need
Let us end this kind of exploitation

WHAT WE CAN DO

LOVE OR FEAR

For every thought processed
An action is expressed
A choice we say
What it is to give away
A choice we do
Things with or without a clue
The manifestation can easily tell
Whether the intention
is from heaven or from hell

Love and fear is influential
Your choice is crucial
Everywhere I go
I am always to know
I see traces of tears
I feel someone's fear
I hear a cry for someone's dear

Few places I know, I sense some cheer
Happiness is clear
Screaming peace and love I feel
Love with which I just want to deal

Trepidation is all over our nation
In this we shouldn't function
Co-creator of God you should stand
Firmly work and act hand in hand
So love can be grand

How do you want to live?
What do you want to feel?
On fear will you rely?
In love, will you defy?

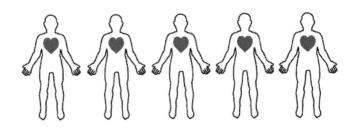

LOVE

The nature of all beings
It never ceases
The basis of all
It is beyond words

It closes the gap
It opens and welcomes all
It heals the wound
It eases all kinds of pain

It softens the hardest of the hearts
It brings out beauty and good
It forgets the differences
It has no gender, no color,
no shapes and sizes

It exposes and rejoices in truth
It never judges, never condemns
It understands the most difficult
It is boundless, limitless, and naked

WE ARE LOVE-D

SELF-LOVE

The greatest love
The most forgotten love
The taken-for-granted love
The taken-out-of-context love
The difficult-to-master love

In its incessant absence
Hatred rules the earth
Judgment is present
Separation in men is evident

In this world of polarity
One cannot exist without the other
If hatred can be given away
So can love

Come back to love, oh beautiful men
For so long you have lived in hate
No more blaming yourselves
Allow yourselves to love again
As your nature has always been love

Self-love
You forgive you for what you are
You accept you for who you are
You see you and in each and everyone
You unite with other souls
A love that is significant to men

104

MY BODY, MY BUDDY, MY RESPONSIBILITY

I listen to your self-talk
I am one with your beliefs
I react to your feelings
I am happy when you're eating
I react to all your doings

I could not breathe in deleterious words
I shake in damaging beliefs
I tremble in pain, stress,
anxiousness, and hate
I get sick eating carcasses
I feel poisoned in drinking
firewater and ardent spirits
I ache and welt in physical abuses

I love you back when you talk to me in love
I am thrilled when you believe in love
I love when you love
I feel whole with the
scrumptiousness of the harvest
I get stronger when you breathe and stretch
I relax in the freshness of
the oceans and seas
Thank you for taking time to surround me with loving
people and nature
I appreciate you for loving me
as you love yourself

WORDS

Alphabets combined become words
Words said create meaning
Meanings and tones invite reaction
Between two or more comes an interaction

Words can change one's life course
Relationships can grow and some can die
People can be loved and can be damaged
The world can see the truth or live with a lie

We can season words with love
or mix them with rage
Depends on how the heart
and mind communicate
You can add meaning or you can eradicate
You and I have a duty to create
To fill the world with words
of love and not of hate

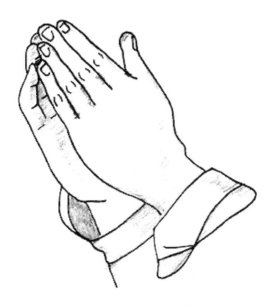

GRATITUDE

Another day
I closed my eyes
I took a deep breath
I mumbled, I sighed
Suddenly my tears rolled down
My cheeks felt its warmth
My heart started to pound

Tired of wanting
I started thanking
As for so many years
The wanting never stopped
I have been forgetting
That the more wants I send out
None of what I want comes in
When my thanking started
The more thanking I see and feel

I wonder if humanity
Is always wanting
Forgetting the thanking
I wonder if humanity
Is realizing
That the universe responds
To whatever we are thinking and feeling

I wonder if humanity
Is recognizing
That nothing is lacking
I wonder if humanity

Is discovering
The power of each being
To shift the consciousness of lack
To a consciousness of abundance
It is time to have an attitude
and prayer of gratitude
And experience the universe's
prosperity in multitude

YOU ARE A GIFT

"I don't have much to give"
But your smile can make someone's day
But your presence and company
may heal a lonely soul
But your listening ears
can ease someone's pain
But your encouraging words
can empower someone

"I don't have money to give"
But your home can shield the homeless
But your food can feed someone
a first meal in days
But your coat can warm the cold
But your shoes can cover
someone's sore bare feet

"I don't know what to give"
But your life story can inspire someone
But your book can motivate someone
But your music can make someone happy
But your voice can speak for the silenced

"I don't have enough to give"
But your faith can make
someone believe again
But your understanding can make
someone feel accepted again
But your patience can make
someone see and learn again

But your generosity can give
someone a chance again

"I don't have a lot to give"
But you are the light to someone's darkness
But your prayer can give someone hope
But your love can make someone live again
But you are a gift to someone in need

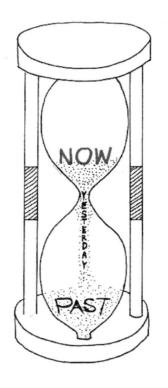

LIVE IN THE NOW

Where else could we be?
Where else could we go?
Where else could we hide?
What else could we have?

It doesn't judge
It doesn't demand
It doesn't mind
It is only still
Only your thoughts unstill

The only place where time is real
The only place where we can feel
The only place where we can know
That everything only exists in the now

MINDFULNESS MEDITATION

When was the last time
You appreciated the day
Waved at a stranger
Observed people without judgment
Did your routine job without complaint
You complimented someone just because
Cooked your food singing
Ate and chewed your food with joy?

When was the last time
You were aware of the present moment
Smelled the flowers
Walked barefoot on the grass
Hugged and thanked an old tree
Listened to the birds chirping
Smiled as the breeze touched your cheeks?

When was the last time
You paused for a while
Stopped and just sighed
Closed your eyes
Realized you're breathing
Felt the surroundings
Emptied your mind
Just sat down and smiled?

In stillness and silence
We can reflect
Connect with the source
Know our higher selves

Find peace
Feel loved
See hope
Lose anxiousness
Gain wisdom

When was the last time you did all these?

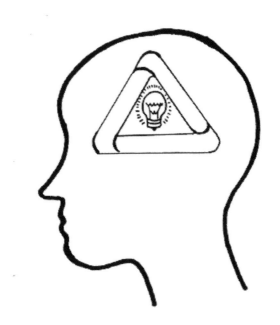

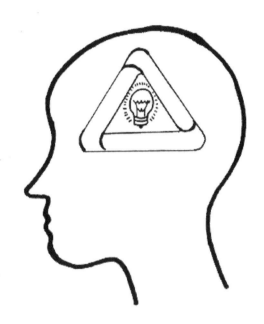

CHANGE MINDSET

I think I can, therefore I could
I think I cannot, therefore I could not
I think I know, therefore I do
I think I don't know, therefore I do not

Whatever I think, becomes
Whenever I think, reveals
Whichever I think, happens
However I think, manifests

Thoughts of love will manifest love
Thoughts of hate will manifest hate
Thousands of thoughts in my head
I am free to choose and set my mind

Your current life can say a lot about you
The status of our world says a lot about us
Challenges in humanity reveals
a lot about you and me
Our thoughts as the collective consciousness
Can tell us how we have become
and how we should be
Let us free our minds from
hatred, anger and greed
May we set our minds for unity and peace
As it brings forth joy,
oneness, love, and ease

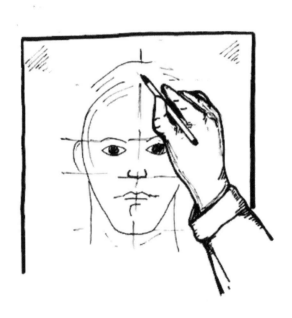

CREATE YOURSELF ANEW

You are a co-creator with
the Divine Intelligence
Every moment, minute, and day,
you may not know
You create, expand and grow
Fueled by your emotions,
thoughts, and desires
Your life is your expression
The result of your creation

For every creation
A story unfolds
Your reality manifests
Expires to your disliking
Till another thought and desire is born
A new life story is written again

Realize your power
What you think
What you desire
What you feel
You create and you become
There is always a new you, every time
A new earth all the time

Create for the good of all
Create for the success of all
Create for the benefit of all
Create for the unity of all
Create for the love of all
Be excited, create in joy,
and create yourself anew

EVOLVE

Humanity, how great we have become
We have sent people to the moon
Have built amazing monuments
Discovered cures for illnesses
Advanced in technologies
Made new breakthroughs
We have done great so far

We have evolved for so long
Yet we are still faced with challenges
We have not fully met the basic principles
Principles of oneness, enoughness,
and beingness

Decide that we are all one
Change the way we treat each other
Decide that there is more than enough
Realize the abundance and share
everything with everyone
Decide that we are human beings
and not human doings
In the state of beingness,
our challenges disappear

Blessed beings of this land
Remember who you truly are
Givers to the needy
Restorers of the broken
Healers of the sick
Bringers of light

Teachers of the confused
Peacemakers and lovers of mankind
Let us highly evolve again
Re-volve

FREE WILL

What should I eat today?
A bowl of salad or a bowl of rice?
Should I ask God about this?
I decided to eat a bowl of salad

Where should I go today?
To work or to the shopping mall?
Should I ask God about this?
I decided to go to work

Which dress should I wear today?
The black velvet or the red silk?
Should I ask God about this?
I decided to wear the black velvet

Why should I be happy today?
Is it because of my life or my family?
Should I ask God about this?
I decided to be happy without any reason

Who should I hurt back today?
Those who did not support me?
Should I ask God about this?
I decided not to hurt anyone

When should I believe in God?
Tomorrow or next time
depends on the miracle signs
Should I ask God about this?
I decided to believe now

I realized that it has always been me
I realized that it's all
my decisions and doings
I realized that it is I who is responsible
I realized that it is I, not God, who is
to be blamed for problems I created
As I have always been free
To will, to let, to act upon and to choose
Who, what, and how
I want myself, and my life to be
I am the deliberate creator of my reality

WAKE UP HUMANITY

Wake up all men
People of power is who we are
We are part of the Divine
We are gods and goddesses
Created in God's image and likeness
Co-creators of an Infinite Creator
Peacemakers and lovers

Our words can bring life
Our thoughts can create a new world
Our wisdom can teach thousands
Our faith can move mountains

We are the consciousness of our planet
With our prayers and
the meeting of our minds
We can change our challenging situations
We can rise up from
our struggles many times

Loving men of this planet
Wake up, time to activate your powers
The power to heal and to unite
The power to let go of the spite

Wake up and go back
Back to your true nature
The nature of kindness and compassion
Time to realize that we are one
Wake up and know who you really are
Universe, God, and most of all...love

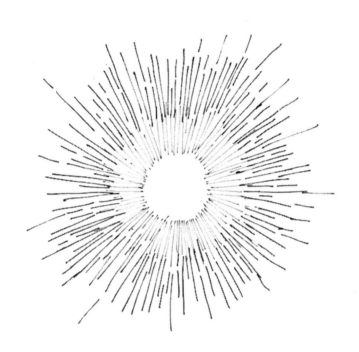

RETURN TO
THE SOURCE

When frightened and worried
Remember that you are peace
When saddened and lonesome
Remember that you are joy
When in scarcity and in need
Remember that you are prosperous
When forgotten and forsaken
Remember that you are love-d

Align yourself with the source
Allow yourself to just be
Let the present moment unfold
Listen to the silence, its guidance
Receive its wisdom, its abundance,
Embrace your true inner being
Be in union, be one again with the source

Blessed being
From soul you originated
To soul you will end
From love you were created
To love you will return
Waste not, fear not, and wander no more
Return to the source
The source is God, the Divine, and the All

WHAT IF AND WHY?

What if you realized that everyone
is just a different version of you?
Will you still judge, hate and compete?
What if everything is just an illusion?
Will you be lost?

What if you discover that
you are also a God?
Will you believe and
stop looking for yourself?
What if you find out that
you are nothing but love?
Will you still hate?

What if you discover
and realized that you are also a saint?
Will you still label yourself as a sinner?
What if you realized that
everything and everyone is holy?
Will you stop judging?

What if there is no God?
Will you still love?
What if you realized that there is no hell place to go to
and rot after you die?
Will you still be afraid and repent?

What if you realized that you are eternal?
Will you welcome death
and stop being afraid?
What if you found out that
there is no judgment?
Will you stop feeling guilty and paranoid?
What if you realized that there is only love?
Will you still live and think in fear?

What if this is your first day to live?
Will you live like you're dying?
What if this is your last day to live?
Will you spend it living?
What if you realized that you come from nothingness,
formlessness and oneness?
Will you still have the same
worries and concerns?

Why do you believe in God?
Why do you not believe in God?
Why do you fear an
unconditional loving God?
Why do you believe and accept the label
that you are rather a sinner than a lover?
Why do you still call yourself imperfect when you know
you were created
by a perfect creator?

Why are you still living in the past
where you know it is already gone?
Why are you living in the present?
Why are you worried about the future
that has not yet come?

Why do you compete with others?
Why do you have to prove yourself?
Why do you have to fight?
Why do you hate someone
that you do not know?

Why do you follow society?
Why do you not listen
and follow your own intuition?
Why do you do what you do
and say what you say?

Why are you happy?
Why are you sad?
Why are you afraid?
Why are you honest?
Why do you lie?
Why do you cheat?
Why do you care?
Why do you love?

WHAT KIND OF A SOURCE ARE YOU?

REQUEST

Kindly leave a review on Amazon after reading this book. Let me know what you have learned and gained from it.

I am inspired to write more books by your reviews. It also helps the book to reach more people and be useful to them.

Thank you so much!

ACKNOWLEDGEMENTS

I would like to thank our Divine Intelligence for inspiring me to write this book.

Thank you too, to my great editor Qat Wanders, my wonderful formatter Jen Henderson, and awesome book cover designer Les who have done an awesome job in making this book possible.

To my incredible launch team, I am inspired by what you do to humanity and I am always touched by your support, a million of thanks to each one of you.

Lastly, to my loving and supportive husband, for his amazing illustrations and for always challenging me to write at my best and take this book to another level.

Thank you, thank you, thank you...

ABOUT THE AUTHOR

 Elsa Mendoza is a Certified Community Life Coach who has a passion for uplifting, empowering, encouraging, motivating, inspiring and helping others to find their passion in life. She helps people identify their strengths and potentials, and change the mindset and old paradigms for a better life and relationship to self and others. Her motivation in doing so is her survival from a harsh family environment during her childhood until her early 20's and overcoming a rare disease that almost took her life. She believes in the power of the human mind, its thoughts and the laws of the universe.

She is always curious, a thinker and a seeker and confident in the power of humanity and the possibility of a much better world where oneness exists.

Elsa is well traveled, has lived in different countries and has interacted with several nationalities, been exposed to different lifestyles, cultures and religions, and has seen what humanity has to offer, thus her inspirations for writing this book.

She holds a Masters of Science Degree in International Business at California International University where she has helped small companies thrive in operations and sales. In her free time, she volunteers at Long Beach Rescue Mission. She loves reading, watching movies, plays, concerts, and traveling with her husband.

ALSO BY
ELSA MENDOZA

You Can Quote Me On This

Words to Empower You and Awaken Your Consciousness

www.amazon.com/dp/B0721HWK3V

To connect with Elsa, she can be reached at elsa@changecreateevolve.com

You can follow her on:

www.facebook.com/elsasvmendoza

www.instagram.com/your_coach_elsa/

www.twitter.com/Lsavm

www.goodreads.com/author/show/16945935.Elsa_Me ndoza

https://partners.bookbub.com/authors/4402533/edit

www.pinterest.com/elsav_mendoza/ boards/

Made in the USA
San Bernardino, CA
20 October 2018